D0090660

Who Was Jesus?

By Ellen Morgan

Illustrated by Stephen Marchesi

Grosset & Dunlap
An Imprint of Penguin Group (USA) LLC

For my mother, my godmother, and my godson—EM

To my parents, Rose and Ennio, whose lives and sacrifices
still inspire—SM

GROSSET & DUNLAP
Published by the Penguin Group
Penguin Group (USA) LLC, 375 Hudson Street, New York, New York 10014, USA

USA | Canada | UK | Ireland | Australia | New Zealand | India | South Africa | China

penguin.com
A Penguin Random House Company

Text copyright © 2015 by Ellen Morgan. Illustrations copyright © 2015 by Stephen Marchesi. Cover illustration copyright © 2015 by Nancy Harrison. All rights reserved. Published by Grosset & Dunlap, a division of Penguin Young Readers Group, 345 Hudson Street, New York, New York 10014. GROSSET & DUNLAP is a trademark of Penguin Group (USA) LLC. Printed in the USA.

Library of Congress Cataloging-in-Publication Data is available.

ISBN 978-0-448-48320-7   10 9 8 7 6 5 4 3 2 1

Contents

Who Was
Jesus?

It's Christmas! Every December 25, all over the world, people are going to church. They gather around Christmas trees. They bake treats. They cook meals for family and friends. They sing songs and open presents.

What is everybody celebrating?

Christmas is the birthday of Jesus. He was born more than two thousand years ago in the small town of Bethlehem. He was from a poor family and grew up to be a preacher. He talked about God and how people should live their lives. He became well-known, and his friends passed along stories about him. They shared his teachings with others.

THE BIBLE

THE BIBLE IS THE HOLY BOOK FOR CHRISTIANS. IT HAS TWO PARTS—THE OLD TESTAMENT AND THE NEW TESTAMENT. THE OLD TESTAMENT TELLS ABOUT THINGS THAT HAPPENED BEFORE JESUS WAS BORN, INCLUDING THE STORIES OF ADAM AND EVE, NOAH'S ARK, AND MOSES. THE NEW TESTAMENT TELLS STORIES ABOUT JESUS AND WHAT HAPPENED AFTER HE DIED. THE OLD TESTAMENT, ESPECIALLY THE FIRST FIVE BOOKS, IS HOLY IN THE JEWISH RELIGION. THESE FIVE BOOKS ARE CALLED THE TORAH.

Jesus's ideas became a movement. The movement started with only a handful of people. But it grew into one of the most important religions in the world—Christianity. Christianity spread to all parts of the globe. Today, there are two billion Christians. They are from different backgrounds, different races, and different cultures, but they share common beliefs.

Christians believe in one God. They believe in Heaven, in life after death. They also believe that Jesus was much more than a preacher. They believe he was the son of God.

THE GOSPELS

MOST OF WHAT PEOPLE LEARN ABOUT THE LIFE OF JESUS COMES FROM THE FIRST FOUR BOOKS IN THE NEW TESTAMENT. THE BOOKS MATTHEW, MARK, LUKE, AND JOHN ARE CALLED THE GOSPELS. (MOST OF THE ACCOUNTS IN THIS BOOK ARE BASED ON THE GOSPELS OF MATTHEW, MARK, LUKE, AND JOHN.) GOSPEL MEANS "GOOD NEWS." THE GOSPELS WERE ALL WRITTEN MANY YEARS AFTER JESUS'S DEATH. SOME PEOPLE BELIEVE MATTHEW AND JOHN WERE JESUS'S DISCIPLES OR FOLLOWERS. OTHER PEOPLE FEEL IT IS DOUBTFUL THAT ANY OF THE WRITERS OF THE GOSPELS KNEW JESUS OR HAD HEARD HIM SPEAK. MOST SCHOLARS THINK THE BOOK OF MARK WAS THE FIRST ONE, WRITTEN AROUND 70 AD. THE BOOKS OF MATTHEW AND LUKE WERE PROBABLY BASED ON WHAT HAD ALREADY BEEN WRITTEN IN THE BOOK OF MARK. JOHN WAS WRITTEN LAST, AROUND 100 AD.

MATTHEW

MARK

LUKE

JOHN

Chapter 1
A Humble Birth

Jesus was born into a Jewish family over two thousand years ago. His father was a carpenter named Joseph. His mother was named Mary.

According to the Gospel of Luke, the angel
Gabriel came to Mary months before Jesus's
birth. "Do not be afraid, Mary," the angel said,
"for you have found favor with God." He told her
she was going to give birth to a special baby boy.

The baby was the son of God, not the son of her
husband, Joseph. Gabriel also told her the baby's
name—Jesus.

Joseph and Mary lived in a region ruled by the Romans and Emperor Augustus. It was called Judea. Right before Jesus was born, Joseph and Mary had to travel to the town of Bethlehem.

EMPEROR AUGUSTUS

The government wanted to register the names of all people living in the area.

WHERE WAS JESUS BORN?

ACCORDING TO THE GOSPELS, JESUS WAS BORN IN BETHLEHEM IN AN AREA OF THE ROMAN EMPIRE CALLED JUDEA. JUDEA STRETCHED FROM THE MEDITERRANEAN SEA TO THE JORDAN RIVER. IT INCLUDED THE CITY OF JERUSALEM. DURING JESUS'S TIME, MOST OF THE PEOPLE IN JUDEA WERE JEWISH. FOR THEM, JERUSALEM WAS THE MOST HOLY CITY IN THE WORLD. AFTER JOSEPH, MARY, AND JESUS RETURNED FROM EGYPT, THEY LIVED IN NAZARETH. (NAZARETH WAS NORTH OF JUDEA, BY THE SEA OF GALILEE.) THAT'S WHY JESUS IS SOMETIMES CALLED JESUS OF NAZARETH.

In Bethlehem, Mary gave birth to her son.

The family stayed in a stable, because the local inn had no room for them. Instead of a crib, Jesus slept in a manger. A manger is a wooden bin that holds food for horses and other animals.

It was a humble start. However, right away, people learned of this birth and knew the baby was special. According to the Gospel of Luke, shepherds in the fields saw an angel above them.

"I am bringing you good news of great joy . . . ," the angel said. He told them a baby had been born who would be the Messiah. *Messiah* is a word for a special person who will save people from great danger or harm.

The Gospel of Matthew says that far away, in a country to the east, three wise men spotted a bright star in the sky. The wise men studied the heavens and understood the star was an important sign.

It meant the Messiah had been born. So they followed the star to Bethlehem to see the baby Jesus.

When the three wise men saw Mary and the baby Jesus, they fell to their knees. They brought him gifts, too—gold, as well as frankincense and myrrh, which were costly spices.

Herod, the king of Judea, also heard about Jesus. The news of Jesus's birth worried Herod.

He asked the wise men to tell him where Jesus was. He told them he just wanted to see the baby, too. But after they had seen the child, a dream warned the wise men to not return to Herod, and instead they went home.

THE ROMAN EMPIRE

BY JESUS'S TIME, THE ROMANS CONTROLLED
A HUGE EMPIRE (SHOWN IN WHITE ON THE MAP).
IT INCLUDED MODERN-DAY ITALY, SPAIN, FRANCE,
PARTS OF NORTHERN AFRICA, AND SYRIA. IT ALSO
INCLUDED JUDEA, WHERE JESUS WAS BORN.
ROMAN LEADERS WORKED HARD TO HOLD THIS
VAST LAND TOGETHER. EACH PART OF THE EMPIRE
HAD ITS OWN GOVERNOR.

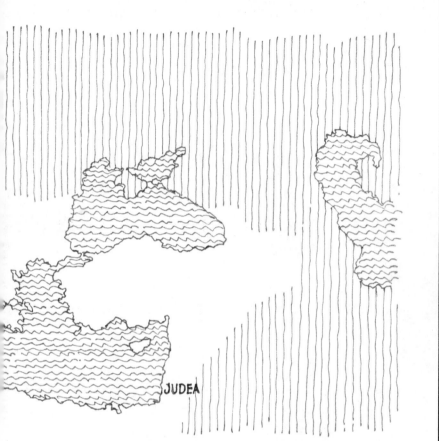

JUDEA

THE GOVERNORS COLLECTED HEAVY TAXES AND USED SOLDIERS TO KEEP ORDER. LAND WAS TAKEN AWAY FROM LANDOWNERS. PEOPLE DID NOT HAVE MANY CIVIL RIGHTS. TROUBLEMAKERS WERE OFTEN KILLED IN PUBLIC. THIS BRUTAL CONTROL SCARED PEOPLE AND ALSO LED TO UNREST. MANY OF THE PEOPLE IN JUDEA WERE POOR, UNHAPPY, AND TROUBLED.

Joseph, Mary's husband, also had a dream. It alerted him that Jesus was in danger. He took Mary and his son and fled at night into the country of Egypt.

Chapter 2
Jesus Grows Up

Not much is known about Jesus's childhood. He may have had several brothers and sisters, including one named James.

Jesus probably went to school from the time he was around six until he was about twelve. All Jewish boys, rich or poor, could go to school. Jewish girls, on the other hand, stayed at home.

School for Jesus most likely took place at the local place of worship. Jewish people called their houses of prayer "synagogues." Jesus's teacher might have been a religious teacher—a rabbi. Jesus would have learned to read Hebrew. He probably spoke Hebrew, as well as another language, Aramaic.

Most of his studies would have been about the
Jewish religion.

In the Gospels, only one story is told about Jesus's childhood. He was twelve at the time of the story. Every year, Jesus's family went to Jerusalem for Passover. Passover was an important holy festival. It honored the Jewish people's escape from slavery in Egypt hundreds of years earlier. Jews were expected to go to Jerusalem for Passover to worship at the great Holy Temple there.

At the end of Passover, Joseph and Mary left
the city to return home to Nazareth. They were
among a large group of people. After they had
started out, they realized their son was not with
them. Worried, Joseph and Mary returned to
Jerusalem. They searched all over for the boy.
At last, they found him, three days later, in the
Temple.

He was sitting in the middle of a group of Jewish
teachers, listening and asking questions. Everyone
who heard him was amazed. For such a young boy,
he understood the Jewish religion so well.

THE TEMPLE

THE TEMPLE IN JERUSALEM SAT ON THE SITE OF AN EARLIER TEMPLE THAT HAD BEEN DESTROYED. DURING JESUS'S TIME, IT WAS HUGE,

LARGER THAN TWENTY FOOTBALL FIELDS. JEWISH
LEADERS RAN THE TEMPLE AND COLLECTED TEMPLE
TAXES. THEY OVERSAW THE RELIGIOUS LIVES
OF THE JEWISH PEOPLE. UNDER THE ROMANS,
JEWISH LEADERS HAD LITTLE POWER. THEY HAD
TO WORK WITH THE ROMANS TO KEEP THE PEACE.
IN THE TEMPLE, THEY STORED SACRED WRITINGS
AS WELL AS LEGAL AND HISTORICAL RECORDS.
PEOPLE CAME THERE TO WORSHIP GOD AND TO
LEARN AND TALK ABOUT RELIGION. IN 70 AD, THE
ROMANS DESTROYED THE TEMPLE. TODAY THE
WESTERN WALL IS ALL THAT REMAINS. IT IS
A HOLY SITE FOR JEWISH PEOPLE, WHO COME
THERE TO PRAY.

Jesus's mother, Mary, was upset, though. "Your father and I have been searching for you," she told him.

Jesus asked, "Why were you searching for me? Did you not know that I must be in my Father's house?" The Temple was the house of God. So Jesus was saying that God was his father.

Years passed, and Jesus grew into a man. During this time, he may have worked as a carpenter, like Joseph. When he was around thirty, Jesus left Nazareth.

He went looking for a man called John. According to the Gospel of Luke, John was Jesus's cousin.

John was also a preacher. When people came to him, he would dip them into the Jordan River and bless them. This ceremony was called "baptism." It was a way to show that a person's sins were being washed away. John became known as John the Baptist.

Jesus found John by the river. There John baptized him. As Jesus came out of the water, he saw the spirit of God over him. He heard a voice speak. "This is my Son, the Beloved," it said.

Afterward, Jesus went into the desert for forty days and forty nights. In many cultures, a trip into a wilderness was a common test for young men. They traveled alone into a wild or harsh place to pray or think.

When Jesus left the desert, he was ready to begin preaching, too.

Chapter 3
Twelve Loyal Men

Jesus had a special message that he wanted to share through his preaching. Under Roman rule, many Jewish people suffered. Jesus offered them a glimpse of a different life. He told them that the kingdom of God was coming soon. God was always with them. To him, the kingdom of God was much more important than the empire of Rome. In the kingdom of God, everyone was equal—rich or poor, strong or weak. Jesus preached a message of love and fairness, of justice and forgiveness.

This was a very new and different idea. Most preachers warned of God's anger and disappointment in people who did not obey God's word. They warned that God would punish sinners. Jesus was different. First he asked people to be sorry for what they had done wrong. Then he spoke of God's love, understanding, and forgiveness.

As he wandered the country, people began
to listen to him. They liked what he had to say.
Large crowds came to hear the young preacher.
They flocked to listen to his lessons, like sheep
to a shepherd.

At one point during his travels, Jesus was walking by the Sea of Galilee. He saw two brothers fishing and called out to them. Their names were Peter and Andrew. "Follow me," he said. He told them that instead of casting their lines for fish, he would make them fishers of men. By this, he meant they would bring in people to hear and believe in what Jesus was preaching. Peter and Andrew left their nets and followed him.

Later, Jesus spotted two other brothers, James and John, on a boat with their father. He called out to them, too. James and John joined Jesus to spread his message.

THE TWELVE DISCIPLES

WHO WERE THE TWELVE DISCIPLES? THEIR NAMES ARE GIVEN IN THREE OF THE GOSPELS— MATTHEW, MARK, AND LUKE.

PETER IS MENTIONED THE MOST IN THE GOSPELS. HE WAS OFTEN THE SPOKESMAN FOR THE TWELVE DISCIPLES.

ANDREW, PETER'S BROTHER, WAS A FOLLOWER OF JOHN THE BAPTIST BEFORE JESUS CALLED HIM.

ALONG WITH PETER AND JOHN, *JAMES* WAS ONE OF THE DISCIPLES CLOSEST TO JESUS.

JOHN WAS JAMES'S BROTHER. HE IS SOMETIMES CALLED "THE DISCIPLE JESUS LOVED."

PHILIP PROBABLY CAME FROM THE SAME TOWN AS PETER AND ANDREW.

SOME SCHOLARS BELIEVE *BARTHOLOMEW* WAS DESCENDED FROM ROYALTY.

MATTHEW WAS A TAX COLLECTOR BEFORE HE BECAME A DISCIPLE.

THOMAS IS USUALLY REMEMBERED FOR DOUBTING THAT JESUS HAD RISEN FROM THE DEAD.

JAMES IS SOMETIMES CALLED "JAMES THE LESS" SO HE ISN'T CONFUSED WITH JAMES, THE BROTHER OF JOHN.

THADDEUS WAS THE BROTHER OF JAMES THE LESS.

SIMON IS ALSO KNOWN AS SIMON THE ZEALOT. ZEALOTS WERE PART OF A JEWISH GROUP THAT HATED ROMAN RULE.

JUDAS ISCARIOT BETRAYED JESUS.

JESUS HAD MANY OTHER FOLLOWERS, BUT THESE TWELVE WERE CLOSEST TO HIM.

HIS FEMALE FOLLOWERS INCLUDED MARY MAGDALENE, MARTHA, JOANNA, AND SUSANNA. SOME PEOPLE BELIEVE THAT HIS MOTHER, MARY, ALSO FOLLOWED HIM WHEN HE WAS PREACHING.

In this way, Jesus gathered a group of twelve loyal followers. They were his disciples. Several women followed Jesus as well. This was unusual at the time. Back then, women did not have the same rights as men. Under Roman law, their husbands and fathers controlled all money and land. In the Temple, women were not allowed into the same areas as men.

Jesus loved and accepted everyone equally, male or female, rich or poor. He felt they all had a place in the kingdom of God.

Chapter 4
Lessons and Stories

Jesus gave many sermons, or lessons. His most famous sermon was preached on a mountain. First he said that people were blessed. "Blessed are the poor. . . . Blessed are the merciful. . . . Blessed are the pure in heart for they will see God . . ."

These messages held out hope, especially to people who hated being under Roman rule. Toward the end of this sermon, Jesus summed up the most important idea. "In everything, do to others as you would have them do to you," he said. Today we call this the Golden Rule.

Jesus also liked to answer people's questions with short stories. These stories are called "parables."

Parables were well suited to the people who came to hear Jesus speak. They were stories about farmers and shepherds, about sons and fathers and neighbors. They were stories about the natural world.

The parable of the Sower is a simple story. But it had an important message. In it, Jesus told about a farmer who went out to plant some seeds. Some of the seeds fell on a path, and birds ate them. Some fell on rocky ground. Although they grew quickly, they died because there was not enough dirt.

Some of the seeds fell on good soil and grew into a big crop.

In this story, the seeds stood for the lessons Jesus was teaching. The ground stood for the people who listened to him. Jesus was asking for people to be like the good soil. He wanted them to listen and understand so that his words would grow and spread.

Jesus often told people to love their neighbors. During another sermon, a lawyer asked Jesus, "Who is my neighbor?" Instead of answering directly, Jesus told this story:

A man from Jerusalem was on a journey when robbers attacked him. They beat him and stole his things, then left him by the side of the road. Several people passed by. They saw the hurt man but didn't help him. Then a man from an area called Samaria came down the road. Most Jewish people and Samaritans were enemies. But that did not stop the Samaritan from helping the man. He took him to an inn and gave the innkeeper money. He asked the innkeeper to care for the man until he was better. If the innkeeper ran out of money, the Samaritan promised to bring him more.

After the story was over, Jesus asked the lawyer who the good neighbor was. The lawyer answered, "The one who showed mercy."

Jesus said, "Go and do likewise."

Jesus told many parables in his teachings, but the Sower and the Good Samaritan were two of the most well-known. People heard these stories and understood what he was saying about the right way to live.

Chapter 5
Jesus the Healer

As more people followed Jesus, the news spread that he could help people in need. Sick people believed he could make them well.

By this time, Jesus also had enemies. They looked for ways to prove he was a fake. On the Sabbath—Saturday—which is the holy day of the week for Jewish people, a man came to Jesus. He had a withered hand and wanted to be healed. Everyone watched carefully. Jews were not supposed to do work on the Sabbath, not even healing. Would Jesus help the man?

It was almost like a trick question. If Jesus helped the man, he would be breaking God's law. He would be doing work on the Sabbath. But if he didn't help the man, he would be ignoring someone in need.

Jesus did not think twice. According to the
Book of Mark, he said, "Stretch out your hand."
When the man did, his hand was better.

Word spread of Jesus's deeds. While he was
preaching, a man named Jairus begged Jesus
to come to his house. Jairus's twelve-year-old
daughter was close to death. Jesus did not make
it in time. The girl had died. At the house, the
people wailed and wept.

Jesus went over to the girl. He took her hand
and said, "Little girl, get up!" Right away, the girl
stood and walked. Everyone was amazed.

This story is told in three of the Gospels—Matthew, Mark, and Luke. Like Jesus's healing of the man's hand, the waking of the dead girl was a miracle. A miracle is something that happens despite the fact that it seems impossible.

In the years that Jesus preached, he healed many people, but he refused to take credit. He said that healing came from God. He also said that the sick person's faith in God made them well again.

Chapter 6
Miracles

During the next few years, more and more people followed Jesus. Often these people were not rich. They did not have a lot of money or a high rank in society. But they believed in Jesus. They believed he could perform miracles.

In addition to healing people, Jesus performed other miracles. His very first miracle took place at a wedding, according to the Gospel of John.

Jesus and his disciples were there. So was his mother, Mary. During the wedding feast, the hosts ran out of wine.

"They have no wine," Mary said to her son. Then she told the servants, "Do whatever he tells you."

Jesus said to them, "Fill the jars with water."

 The servants filled the jars to the brim. Jesus asked them to take the jars to the wine steward. The steward tasted it. The water had become wine!

What happened was considered a miracle, just like healing the man with the withered hand or bringing Jairus's daughter back to life.

Another time, Jesus and the disciples went to a deserted place to rest. Many people saw them going. They knew who Jesus was and went along.

Jesus decided to preach to them. Soon five

thousand people had gathered. When it grew late, Jesus's disciples suggested that they send the people away to buy food. To their surprise, Jesus told the disciples to feed the people. But how? The disciples did not have enough supplies to feed five thousand people!

Jesus asked his disciples to collect as much food as they could find. But all they brought back were five loaves of bread and two fish.

Jesus said a blessing over the bread and the fish. Then he broke the food into pieces. He gave them to his disciples to pass out to the people. Amazingly, there was enough to feed all the people in the crowd until everyone was full. Afterward, the disciples gathered up the leftovers. They filled twelve baskets with what hadn't been eaten! This was another miracle. It was a sign of Jesus's—and God's—power.

As all the people left, Jesus told his disciples to board a ship. He would meet them on the other side of the sea. According to the Gospel of Matthew, Jesus went by himself up a mountain to pray. Night fell. At sea, the wind began to blow hard. The disciples had trouble steering the ship. As they struggled, they looked out and were shocked to see someone coming toward them. He was walking on the water!

At first, they were scared. Had they seen a ghost? Then the man called out to them. "Take heart, it is I. Do not be afraid." It was Jesus!

Peter answered him, "Lord, if it is you, command me to come to you on the water."

Jesus said, "Come."

So Peter left the ship and did what Jesus asked.
He began to walk on the water toward Jesus. But
Peter felt the wind and the waves and became
scared. He was starting to sink when Jesus reached
out and caught him.

"You of little faith, why did you doubt?" Jesus said. With that, the wind stopped blowing, and the sea was calm. And they returned to the ship. What Jesus meant was that Peter would have kept walking on the water if his belief in Jesus had been stronger.

What happened at sea was considered another miracle. During Jesus's life, many people saw him perform miracles, but miracles were just one reason people followed him. Jesus's message of love and the kingdom of God gave them hope, too.

For hundreds of years, people had heard stories that one day a man would free the Jewish people from their enemies. This person was known as the Messiah or "anointed one." (That means a person who has been specially chosen by God.) The Greek word for "anointed" is "Christos," or Christ. That is why Jesus became known as Jesus Christ.

Some people thought the Messiah would be a king. Some people thought he would be a priest.

Many expected a great warrior. Jesus was certainly no warrior. His message was the opposite of war and violence. He preached about peace. Still, many people during his time believed he might be the person to free them, at last, from the Romans.

Chapter 7
Enemies

Jesus had enemies. Not everyone liked what he was preaching. Some people felt threatened by his words. He said things that some people did not want to hear. To Jesus, wealth and a high standing in society did not equal greatness. If you were a bad person, all your success did not

mean anything. Rich people thought Jesus liked the poor better. At one point, he even said it was easier for a camel to pass through the eye of a needle than for a rich man to enter the kingdom of God.

Some Jewish leaders saw Jesus as a threat. His followers called him the Messiah and the son of God. To Jewish leaders, that seemed wicked and disrespectful of God. God did not have a son. Jesus broke many Jewish laws to uphold what he thought was a more important law—to love your neighbor. He healed the sick on the Sabbath.

Jesus also threatened the uneasy balance between the Romans and the Jewish people, who were under Roman rule. Jesus was saying things that the Romans didn't like. He was saying the only true power came from God. Would they blame the Jews for Jesus's words? Would they take it out on the Jewish people?

Indeed, many Romans saw Jesus as a threat. They felt he was a troublemaker. Everywhere he went, huge crowds gathered. The Romans worried that Jesus's followers would revolt against their empire.

Jesus knew people were plotting against him. Many of his enemies were in Jerusalem—rich people, Jewish leaders, and Romans. The special Jewish holy festival of Passover was coming up. Usually Jewish people went to Jerusalem for Passover to worship at the Temple. Jesus was in Galilee at the time. He could have stayed there where he was safe. Instead he decided to travel to Jerusalem for the festival.

Before starting the trip, Jesus brought his disciples together. He gave them a warning. He was going to be betrayed. He was going to be sentenced to death. People would mock him and beat him and spit on him. He would be hung on a cross, and he would die. On the third day after his death, he would rise again.

In this way, Jesus predicted his own death. His disciples, though, did not believe it. They loved him so much. They could not imagine a world without him.

Chapter 8
Palm Sunday

When Jesus and the disciples got close to Jerusalem, Jesus sent two of them ahead. He told them they would find a donkey in a nearby town. "Untie it and bring it here," he said.

The disciples went into the town and did as Jesus asked. A man stopped them. He wanted to know why they were untying the donkey.

Jesus had told the two disciples that this might happen. He had given them an answer. "The Lord needs it," they said, and went on their way.

The disciples took the donkey to Jesus. They laid their cloaks over it. Then Jesus sat on the donkey's back.

As he rode into Jerusalem, people greeted him with praises. They tossed branches of palm trees in his path. In Greek and Roman culture, palm branches were a symbol for victory.

In Jerusalem, high on the Temple Mount,
was the Temple. The Temple was not only a place
of worship. It was the center of Jewish life. Many
people worked there. It was a busy
marketplace. People also came to
the Temple to pay the Temple tax.
Only one type of money was used
to pay this tax.

When Jesus arrived at the Temple in Jerusalem,
what he saw there made him very angry. The
Temple should have been a holy place, a place to
pray to God. Instead it appeared to be a place of

business. In Jesus's eyes, the people there had taken a house of prayer and "made it a den of robbers."

Jesus overturned the tables where people exchanged Roman and foreign money for coins to pay the Temple tax. He threw out the people who were selling things.

Jesus was a peaceful man. He preached a message of love and tolerance. This time at the Temple is one of the only instances in the New Testament where he loses his temper.

Chapter 9
Jesus's Last Supper

Passover came a few days after Jesus lost his temper in the Temple, and he wanted to spend the first evening with his disciples. He brought the twelve of them together in a large room in a house in Jerusalem. They sat down to have a seder—the Passover meal—together. It was to be Jesus's

Last Supper. According to the Gospel of Mark, as they ate, Jesus said to them, "Truly I tell you, one of you will betray me."

The disciples were shocked. Who would betray Jesus? Each said, "Surely, not I?"

Jesus insisted that "It is one of the twelve." He did not say who. He did not seem angry. Jesus blessed the bread and the wine, and the seder continued.

At the end of the seder, Jesus said, "I will never again drink of the fruit of the vine"—by that he meant wine—"until that day when I drink it new in the kingdom of God." He knew that his enemies were gathering. He knew he would die soon.

Afterward, Jesus and the disciples left the room and went to the Mount of Olives. There Jesus gave them another warning. He told them that they would desert him in the coming days.

Peter protested—he would never desert Jesus! Jesus insisted that by the next morning, before a rooster had crowed, Peter would deny three times that he knew him.

Jesus led his disciples to a garden. He wanted
to pray by himself, but he knew death would be
coming soon, so he wanted his friends nearby. He
took three of them—Peter, James, and John—
close to the spot where he intended to pray.

According to the Gospel of Mark, he told these three disciples, "Remain here and keep awake." But while Jesus was praying, the disciples fell asleep. "Could you not keep awake one hour?" Jesus asked. Two more times, he went back to pray.

Two more times, he found his friends asleep on his return. The last time, he told them, "Get up, let us be going. See, my betrayer is at hand."

It was true!

Judas, one of Jesus's disciples, was waiting for him outside the garden. Judas had shared the seder meal with Jesus. But now Judas had turned on his teacher. Jesus's enemies had paid Judas thirty silver coins. With Judas were Roman guards and a crowd of people with swords and staffs.

Judas came to Jesus and gave him a kiss. This was a sign to the guards. Jesus was the troublemaker they were looking for. With that kiss, Judas betrayed Jesus. The guards grabbed Jesus, who did not resist. They brought him to the high priest.

The high priest held a trial. Jesus's crime
was that he claimed to be the son of God.
During the trial, many people in the crowd lied.
They said they had heard Jesus say he would
destroy the Temple.

Peter had followed Jesus at a safe distance.
He sat with some servants of the high priest. He
warmed himself by their fire. A servant girl said
to Peter, "You also were with Jesus." She had seen
them together before. But Peter was scared. So he
denied knowing Jesus. As one of Jesus's disciples,
he was in danger, too. Peter was trying to lie low.
He was trying to protect himself.

Then, twice more, other people accused Peter of
being a follower of Jesus. Each time, Peter denied it.

Just as he said, "I do not know this man you are talking about," a rooster crowed.

All of a sudden, Peter remembered Jesus's words to him—that Peter would deny being a disciple—and he wept.

He had betrayed the man he held so dear.

The trial ended.

The high priest had found Jesus guilty of claiming to be the son of God.

Chapter 10
Pontius Pilate

The high priest did not have the power to sentence Jesus to death. The Romans were the rulers of the land. So Jesus was brought before Pontius Pilate. Pilate was the Roman governor of Judea.

The Romans did not care about Jesus being called the son of God. They were worried that Jesus might cause his followers to rebel against the Romans.

Jesus was put on trial again. This time it was in

a Roman court. The charges were different. Jesus had tried to get people to riot, they said. He had ·claimed to be a king.

"Are you the king of the Jews?" Pontius Pilate asked him. Claiming to be a king was dangerous. A king was a threat to the power of the Roman Empire.

Jesus did not deny it. But he did not say yes, either.

What should Pontius Pilate do? There was a custom that a prisoner could be set free in honor of the Passover feast. Pilate asked the people if they wanted him to set Jesus free. No, they said. Instead they asked that another man, who was a murderer, be let go.

So Pontius Pilate sentenced Jesus to death. He would be killed by crucifixion. He would be hung on a wooden cross by nails through his hands and feet.

Crucifixion was horrible. Some people took days to die. It was a way the Romans killed criminals and rebels. Since crosses were set up outside, people could watch the deaths. It was a warning—this was what happened when people defied the Romans.

Before Jesus's crucifixion, Roman soldiers whipped him and dressed him up like a king.

This was not to honor him. It was to mock him. They placed a crown of thorns on his head. In one of Jesus's hands, they put a staff. "Hail, king of the Jews," they teased. They spit at him. They beat him. Then they took him to a hill called Golgotha.

Jesus was hung on a cross to die. At the top of the cross was a sign that said "Jesus of Nazareth, King of the Jews." This was mocking him, as well. Two thieves were also crucified that day, one on either side of him. As he suffered, people continued to mock Jesus. They had heard he could work miracles. "Save yourself," they said.

All the Gospels mention that some of Jesus's female followers were there at Golgotha. The Gospel of John says that Mary, Jesus's mother, was there, too. How hard it must have been to see her son in such pain!

Even though it was daytime, the sky grew dark. The darkness lasted for three hours. Jesus was in agony. He cried out loud, "My God, my God, why have you forsaken me?"

He gave another cry and passed away.

As he died, the earth shook. Stones broke. A Roman soldier by the cross felt the earthquake and cried out, "Truly this man was God's son!"

JESUS AND OTHER RELIGIONS

CHRISTIANS SEE JESUS AS THE SON OF GOD. TO THEM, HE WAS THE MESSIAH OR "CHRIST." JEWS DO NOT BELIEVE JESUS WAS GOD'S SON, OR A MESSIAH. THEY THINK OF HIM AS A WONDERFUL TEACHER. HIS LESSONS WERE SIMILAR TO THOSE OF JEWISH RABBIS WHO LIVED AT THE SAME TIME.

SOME HINDUS SEE JESUS AS A HUMAN FORM OF THEIR GOD VISHNU. TO MUSLIMS, JESUS, OR "ISSA," WAS A PROPHET. MUSLIMS RESPECT ALL PROPHETS. BUT JESUS HAS A SPECIAL PLACE FOR THEM. THEY BELIEVE HE TOLD OF THE COMING OF MUHAMMAD, WHO FOUNDED THE RELIGION OF ISLAM.

VISHNU

Chapter 11
Jesus Rises

After Jesus died, a rich man named Joseph went to Pontius Pilate. Joseph was a secret follower of Jesus. He asked if he could have Jesus's body in order to bury it. Pilate agreed.

Joseph wrapped the body in clean linen cloth. He laid it in a tomb that had been carved out of rock. A great stone was rolled in front of the tomb's entrance to keep the body safe.

CHRISTIAN SYMBOLS

JESUS'S LIFE GAVE RISE TO MANY CHRISTIAN SYMBOLS. HERE ARE SOME OF THEM AND WHAT THEY MEAN.

FISH: A FISH BECAME A SYMBOL OF CHRISTIANITY FOR SEVERAL REASONS. SOME OF  JESUS'S DISCIPLES WERE FISHERMEN, AND JESUS CALLED HIMSELF A FISHER OF MEN. JESUS ALSO FED FISH AND BREAD TO THE CROWDS.

CROSS: CHRISTIANS BELIEVE THAT JESUS DIED SO HIS FOLLOWERS' SINS—AND THE SINS OF ALL THE PEOPLE AFTER THEM—WOULD BE FORGIVEN. THE CROSS IS A SYMBOL OF HIS SACRIFICE.

PALMS: PALM BRANCHES REMIND CHRISTIANS OF JESUS'S ENTRY INTO JERUSALEM DURING THE FINAL WEEK OF HIS LIFE.

LAMB: SOMETIMES JESUS IS CALLED THE LAMB OF GOD. DURING BIBLICAL TIMES, ANIMALS—OFTEN LAMBS— WERE KILLED AS AN OFFERING TO CLEAR AWAY SIN. BY DYING ON THE CROSS, JESUS HIMSELF WAS A SACRIFICE.

As followers of Jesus, the disciples were in danger. Now many of them fled or went into hiding.

Romans did not see women as threats. Jesus's female followers did not hide like the male disciples. They went to the tomb to mourn.

According to the Gospel of John, on the third day after Jesus died, Mary Magdalene visited the tomb. It was early and still dark. She saw the stone that had sealed the tomb had been rolled away.

Shocked, Mary Magdalene ran from the tomb. She found Peter and another disciple, who had not fled. "They have taken the Lord out of the tomb," she said, "and we do not know where they have laid him."

The disciples hurried to the tomb. It was empty, just as Mary Magdalene had said, except for a linen cloth.

After they left, Mary Magdalene stayed at the

tomb, weeping. She looked into the tomb again
and saw two angels in white. "Woman, why are
you weeping?" they asked. She told them the body
of Jesus was gone.

Suddenly a man spoke to her. "For whom are you looking?" he asked. Then he said her name, and she knew who it was. It was Jesus. He had risen from the dead, just as he had predicted.

Mary Magdalene told the disciples what she had seen. They remembered his words to them. They remembered Jesus had said he would rise on the third day after his death.

That evening in Jerusalem, the disciples came together to talk over what had happened. They met in secret. They shut the doors of the building because they were afraid of being found. Not all of them believed that Mary Magdalene had seen Jesus.

According to the Gospel of John, suddenly a man appeared among them, even though the doors were shut. He was not a soldier, searching for them. He was not a guard, either.

It was Jesus, risen from the dead!

"Peace be with you," he said. He showed them the wounds in his hands and on the side of his body.

One of the disciples, Thomas, was not there with the others. When he heard about Jesus appearing, he did not believe it. "Unless I see the mark of the nails in his hands," he said, "I will not believe."

About a week later, the disciples all came together again. This time, Thomas was with them. Jesus appeared once again and stood among them.

"Put your finger here and see my hands." He was asking Thomas to touch his wounds. "Do not doubt but believe."

Now Thomas, too, believed the miracle.

In the forty days after his death, Jesus appeared to his disciples at different times in different ways. He comforted them, and he instructed them. He gave them faith when, like Thomas, they were not sure what to believe.

After forty days, according to the Gospels, Jesus left the earth behind to go to Heaven. He had a last message for his disciples, though. He wanted his teachings to live on after his death. He wanted the good news of the kingdom of God to spread throughout the world. He said, "Go, therefore, and make disciples of all nations, baptizing them in the name of the Father and of the Son and of the Holy Spirit, and teaching them to obey everything that I have commanded you. And remember, I am with you always, to the end of the age."

CHRISTMAS

JESUS HAS THE MOST FAMOUS BIRTHDAY EVER. HIS BIRTH IS ALSO CALLED THE NATIVITY. NO ONE KNOWS FOR SURE, THOUGH, WHAT DAY HE WAS ACTUALLY BORN. NONE OF THE GOSPELS GIVE A DATE. AROUND 200 AD, SOME PEOPLE BEGAN TO CLAIM DECEMBER 25 AS THE BIRTHDAY OF JESUS. BY 336 AD, THE EARLY CATHOLIC CHURCH AGREED. ON THAT YEAR AND THAT DAY, THE FIRST FEAST OF THE NATIVITY IS RECORDED.

EASTER

EASTER HONORS JESUS'S LAST DAYS ON EARTH. GOOD FRIDAY IS THE DAY JESUS DIED. EASTER SUNDAY IS THE DAY HE ROSE FROM THE DEAD. FOR CHRISTIANS, EASTER IS ABOUT MORE THAN THE MIRACLE OF JESUS OVERCOMING DEATH. HIS WILLING SACRIFICE PAID FOR THE SINS OF ALL PEOPLE. ANYONE WHO BELIEVED IN HIM, BOTH IN HIS TIME AND IN ALL FUTURE CENTURIES, WOULD BE SAVED. WHEN THEY DIED, THEY WOULD GO TO HEAVEN. FOR CHRISTIANS, THIS IS THE ULTIMATE MIRACLE OF JESUS'S LIFE.

Chapter 12
The Early Christians

Jesus's death left his followers in turmoil. Many people had believed he was the Messiah. They had thought he would overthrow the Romans and bring about the kingdom of God on earth, a place where everyone was equal and important. His death, after he had only preached for about three years, was a shock. How could he free them from Roman rule now that he was gone?

When Jesus appeared to the disciples after his death, he asked them to share his teachings. The disciples did this. From then on, they were called "apostles," or messengers.

The apostles spread out to teach about Jesus to anyone who would listen. Many people did listen and believed.

Other people listened and did not like what they heard.

The Romans hounded the apostles. Some were thrown in prison. Some were beaten. Some, like Peter and James, were put to death for spreading Jesus's message.

Still the apostles continued to preach and teach. They traveled many miles and spent their lives spreading the word. The original apostles went as far as today's Greece, Turkey, North Africa, and India. The next generation of followers went even farther.

At first, their message was not viewed as a new religion. Followers of Jesus still saw themselves as Jewish. They worshipped at the Temple and followed Jewish laws. Their beliefs, though, were different in some ways from Jewish beliefs. They believed that Jesus was the Messiah or Christ. They believed that followers of Jesus could find eternal life in Heaven.

This movement began to feel very different from the Jewish religion. Its followers could no longer be considered Jewish. They called themselves Christians, or followers of Christ. More and more people believed Jesus's message. Christianity spread throughout the western world. Finally, around 325 AD, it even became the main religion of the Roman Empire.

At last, through love and sacrifice, Jesus had conquered the Romans.

PETER AND THE CHURCH

JESUS HAD A SPECIAL ROLE IN MIND FOR HIS DISCIPLE PETER. ACCORDING TO THE BOOK OF MATTHEW, JESUS TOLD HIM, "YOU ARE PETER, AND ON THIS ROCK, I WILL BUILD MY CHURCH." JESUS KNEW THAT PETER WAS SOLID, LIKE A ROCK. HE WAS THE RIGHT MAN TO FOUND A NEW KIND OF CHURCH. JESUS'S WORDS WERE ALSO A PUN— THE NAME PETER MEANS "ROCK" IN GREEK. FIFTY DAYS AFTER PASSOVER, THE DISCIPLES AND OTHER FOLLOWERS OF JESUS GATHERED TOGETHER FOR A FEAST. PETER TOLD THE PEOPLE ABOUT JESUS'S DEATH AND HIS RESURRECTION. THESE PEOPLE— ABOUT THREE THOUSAND OF THEM—WERE THEN BAPTIZED. MANY PEOPLE THINK OF THIS DAY, WHICH IS ALSO KNOWN AS PENTECOST, AS THE START OF THE CHRISTIAN CHURCH.

PAUL

THE TWO MOST IMPORTANT LEADERS OF THE EARLY CHRISTIAN MOVEMENT WERE PETER AND PAUL. UNLIKE PETER, PAUL WAS NOT ONE OF JESUS'S DISCIPLES. IN FACT, HE WAS AGAINST EARLY CHRISTIANS AND TRIED TO STAMP OUT THE MOVEMENT. THEN, ON HIS WAY TO ARREST SOME OF JESUS'S FOLLOWERS, HE CHANGED. A BRIGHT LIGHT FROM HEAVEN BLINDED HIM. HE FELL TO THE GROUND AND HEARD A VOICE. IT WAS THE VOICE OF JESUS. "WHY DO YOU PERSECUTE ME?" THE VOICE ASKED. FOR THREE DAYS AFTERWARD, PAUL WAS BLIND AND DID NOT EAT OR DRINK. WHEN HIS SIGHT CAME BACK, HE BEGAN TO TEACH JESUS'S MESSAGE, TOO. PAUL WROTE SEVERAL BOOKS IN THE NEW TESTAMENT. HE TRAVELED AS MANY AS TEN THOUSAND MILES PREACHING. HE BECAME AN IMPORTANT LEADER IN THE EARLY CHURCH. PAUL WAS PUT TO DEATH FOR HIS BELIEFS AROUND 65 AD.

TIMELINE OF JESUS'S LIFE

According to Christian tradition, Jesus was born in the year 0 AD. This idea came from a monk in the sixth century. However, the monk actually made a mistake. Most historians now believe Jesus was born in around 6–4 BC.

63 BC	The Roman Empire takes control of Judea
6–4 BC	Jesus is born
4 BC	Herod dies
26 AD	Pontius Pilate becomes governor in Jerusalem
CA. 28 AD	Jesus baptized by John the Baptist
CA. 30 AD	Jesus dies
37 AD	Pontius Pilate exiled to Gaul
66–70 AD	Jewish rebellion against Roman rule
70 AD	The destruction of the Temple
CA. 65–70 AD	The Gospel of Mark is written
CA. 80–90 AD	The Gospels of Matthew and Luke are written
CA. 90–100 AD	The Gospel of John is written

TIMELINE OF
THE WORLD

Roman general Julius Caesar invades Gaul — **58 BC**

Cleopatra becomes queen of Egypt — **51 BC**

Water-powered bellows and iron furnaces are invented in China — CA. **30 AD**

Romans establish Londinium, present-day London — CA. **50 AD**

Fires destroy half of Rome; Roman emperor Nero blames Christians — **64 AD**

Construction of the Colosseum begins in Rome — **70 AD**

The city of Pompeii is destroyed after Mount Vesuvius erupts — **79 AD**

Paper is first invented in China
Ancestral Pueblo tribe establishes itself in northern Arizona, New Mexico, southern Utah, and Colorado — CA. **100 AD**

The first Mayan temples are completed in Central America — CA. **200 AD**

BIBLIOGRAPHY

* Adams, Simon. **The Story of World Religions**. New York: Rosen Publishing Group, 2012.

Aslan, Reza. **Zealot: The Life and Times of Jesus of Nazareth**. New York: Random House, 2013.

Bloom, Harold. **Jesus and Yahweh: The Names Divine**. New York: Riverhead Books, 2005.

* Corona, Laurel. **Religions of the World: Judaism**. San Diego: Lucent Books, 2003.

* Harik, Ramsay M. **Jesus of Nazareth: Teacher and Prophet**. New York: Franklin Watts, 2001.

Holy Bible: The HarperCollins Study Bible, New Revised Standard Version. New York: HarperCollins, 2006.

* Schippe, Cullen and Chuck Stetson, ed. **The Bible and Its Influence**. New York: BLP Publishing, 2006.

* Whitbread, Henry. **Lives of the Great Spiritual Leaders**. London: Thames & Hudson, 2011.

* Books for young readers